How to play baseball

How to play baseball

By Martin Iger and Robert Fitzsimmons

Doubleday & Company, Inc.   **Garden City, New York**

To Riley, Brian and Stacey

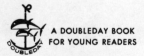
A DOUBLEDAY BOOK
FOR YOUNG READERS

Library of Congress Catalog Card Number 62-15103
Copyright © 1962 by Martin Iger and Robert Fitzsimmons
All Rights Reserved
Printed in the United States of America
First Edition

The sport that gives the most fun to the most people is baseball. It is played by millions of youngsters on sandlots all over the country. A similar game, softball, is played by many people, even after they are old. And young or old, everybody likes to watch **baseball**

Baseball is fun for everyone, but to play it, you must first be able to do three things:

Throw

Catch Hit

Throwing

A baseball player should be able to throw accurately, throw quickly, and throw far. The first thing, though, is to know how to hold the ball.

A baseball is held with only three fingers. The thumb goes on the bottom, and the index and middle fingers are on top, spread slightly apart so that they go along the seams.

Throwing is mostly a matter of keeping at it until you develop good muscles and timing. Muscles have to grow, but you can speed timing along by yourself. One thing you should keep in mind is that you throw with your whole body, not with your arm alone.

Want to prove this?

Stand with your feet together, hold the ball up high, and flip it just by snapping your wrist.

Now, with feet still together and not moving, throw it by using your whole arm. The ball went farther this time.

But now try the same thing, only this time snapping your wrist as you throw with your arm while also stepping forward. The combination of using your body, arm, and wrist made the ball go farther than ever. Now all you have to do is to find the best way to do all these things together.

This is easy if you can remember one word ... Constantinople ...

Con- -stan- -ti- -no- -ple

Got it?

You're starting with the ball at your chest.

You start to drop your arm in the beginning of what will be a giant loop.

Your arm has started its forward swing so that your hand is right behind your ear. Your whole body is starting to move forward fast now, and you are about to release the ball.

Your arm is now straight down toward the ground, you're leaning back, and your front foot is off the ground ready to step forward.

-ple

Con- -stan-
-ti- -no- -ple

Keep saying it as you practice these steps until everything becomes one smooth motion and you will have mastered a difficult secret of throwing...timing.

The ball is gone. But it left your hand with a final snap of the wrist. And with this last motion, your whole body has moved forward so that at the finish, your back foot is up even with your front foot.

In baseball, though, it is much more important to throw accurately than to throw far or throw quickly.

How can you throw more accurately?

One way is to always throw at a specific target. Instead of just throwing "toward" a friend, aim for a spot. Try to hit his right shoulder, or his belt buckle, or his left knee. If you try this all the time, you'll soon be able to come close to any target you want to throw at most of the time.

There's another thing that will help you to throw straight. Watch Riley throwing down the line. See how his feet are lined up with the target?

He's at

Con-

remember?

At stan he is still in line, and notice how he never turns his head away from the target.

At ti he is still in line, even though his weight has shifted to the back foot.

At no his feet, knees, shoulders, and head are still lined up.

At ple Riley's body is coming full forward to face the target and throw all his weight behind the pitch.

He ends up with both feet almost even, and notice how
the ball is sailing straight for its target.

Catching

Everybody who has tried to catch a ball knows that most of the time you miss in the beginning. But like anything else, the more you keep trying, the easier it becomes until you hardly miss at all.

In baseball, there are three different types of gloves to help you catch. One looks like a scoop shovel. It is used by the first baseman to scoop up balls thrown into the dirt...

This is a scoop glove

...sometimes it is used to snag balls thrown high over your head.

The first baseman often has to catch with his one gloved hand, so the scoop glove is shaped like an enormous mitten to trap the ball. Your fingers go into this glove only far enough to make the trap snap shut.

This is a catcher's glove

Another type of glove is the catcher's mitt. This is a big round glove that makes a good target for the pitcher. The round glove is used only by the catcher.

Everybody else uses a more familiar type of glove which has five fingers and is called a fielder's glove.

This is a fielder's glove

The best way to catch is to use both hands whenever you can. Try to make the ball hit the pocket of the glove and use your bare hand to clasp it there tightly.

Besides helping you catch the ball, it leaves you in position
to throw the ball quickly to someone else.

How do you catch a ball hit high into the air, or one that comes racing across the ground?

You should try to get under a ball hit up into the air (called a fly ball) so that you can catch it by reaching up over your head. That way, if it starts to drop out of your hands, you might be able to retrieve the ball before it hits the ground.

A ball hit along the ground (called a grounder) is sometimes difficult to catch because it might be skipping
crazily, or it might hit a pebble and bounce sky-high at
the last moment. Did a grounder ever roll right between
your legs? Didn't you feel foolish?

The best way to catch a grounder is to get right in front of it so that your whole body will block it in case you miss it with your glove.

If there is time, put your knee on the ground alongside of your foot so that there is no chance in the world of the ball going between your legs.

When you become good, you will learn extra things, such as how to hold your glove to shield your eyes from the sun when catching a fly ball. But one final thing you should know right now is how to hold your hands. Always keep them open so that your palms, and not your finger tips, are facing the ball.

After all, if the ball hits your palms, you will catch it. If it hits your finger tips, it will only sting.

Hitting

Most boys like to hit more than catch or throw. But hitting is not quite so simple as it might seem. As in throwing, timing is very important, and it is something that is learned by constant practice.

Of course, you must know the right way to hold a bat. Make a fist with each hand. Now hold your fists together so that eight fingers all line up in a row.

Remembering that position, pick up a bat and grasp it with your hands the same way. This is the proper way to hold a bat. Be sure, though, that you don't hold it right down at the very end. Choke up a little so that some of the wood is showing below your hands and you are able to move the whole bat comfortably with just your wrists.

The most important thing to know about hitting is to

Keep your eye on the ball

Does that sound funny? It shouldn't because how else can you hit a ball if you don't keep your eye on it? Yet the reason most people miss is that they swing so hard that at the last minute—just when the bat is about to hit the ball—not only their eyes, but their head turns away. So one of the best ways to learn to hit is by first learning to bunt.

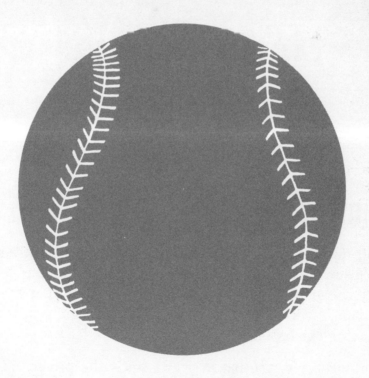

How to bunt

Bunting is simply a matter of tapping the ball lightly so that it dribbles out in front of the batter and on to the playing field. Sometimes a batter is called upon to bunt so that another base runner can advance while the fielders are kept busy going after the ball and getting the batter out at first base.

To bunt properly, the batter waits until the pitcher is about to deliver the ball. Then he swings his back foot around so that his body is facing the pitcher, moves his top hand up to give him greater control of the bat, and tries to hold the bat so that it will be in position to just meet the ball. Since bunting is important, you should practice this often.

How to stand

Except when bunting, you should stand sideways, with only your face pointing toward the pitcher.

Your feet should be in a line, with the bat held way back so that you can bring it around in a mighty swing as you hit the ball.

Just as in throwing, you hit with your whole body. As you swing the bat, the weight of your body moves forward, you snap your wrists so that the bat comes all the way around, and all this time your eye is always on the ball.

See how Riley does it. As the ball comes toward him, he steps forward to meet it.

Notice his level swing. The end of the bat does not point up or down.

As he hits the ball,
he snaps his wrists.

See how he follows through
with his whole body....

...and there it goes   ...and there he goes

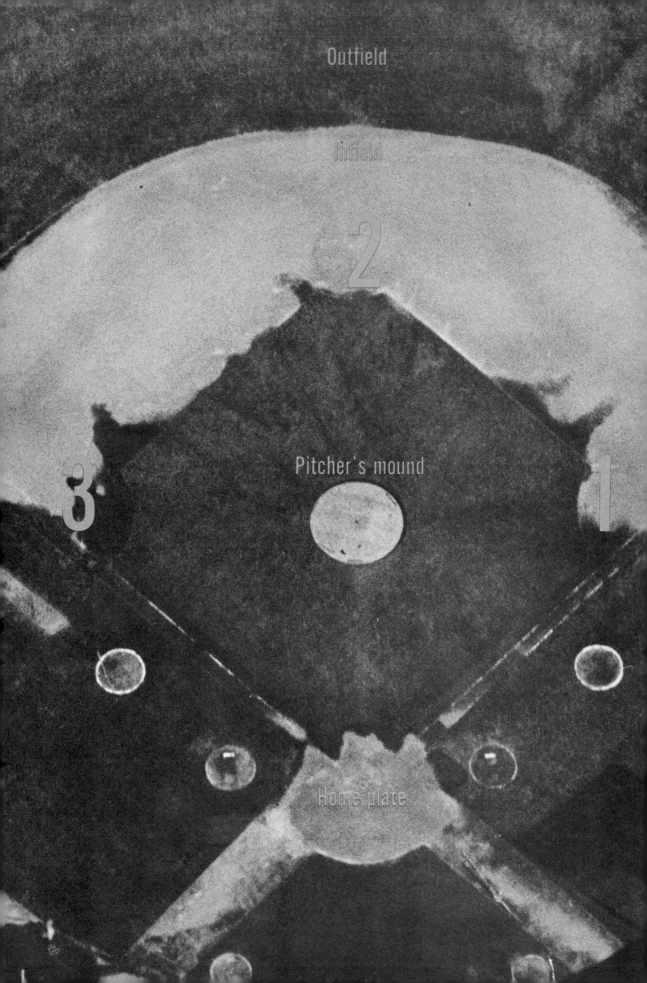

Let's look at the field

Now you know the basic skills of baseball—how to throw, catch, and hit. The next thing you must know is how to play the game itself.

First, let's take a look at the playing field. Notice that it resembles a diamond. In each of its four corners is a base. The base at the bottom of the diamond is called "home plate." That's where the batter stands.

First base is at the right corner of the diamond. Second base is at the far corner opposite home plate. Third base is at the left corner. The area beyond the diamond is called the outfield.

The batter must try to get from home to first, second, third, and back home without being put "out." If he does that, he scores a "run."

Each team has nine players, and each team gets nine chances to bat. After three batters of one team are put "out," the teams change sides—one going to the field while the other hits. A time at bat and a time in the field completes an "inning." There are nine innings in a game. So you see, a team comes up to bat nine times, and each time it is allowed three outs. After each team has taken its nine turns at bat, the one with the most runs wins. If both teams have scored the same number of runs, they each take another turn until one team wins by scoring more runs than the other.

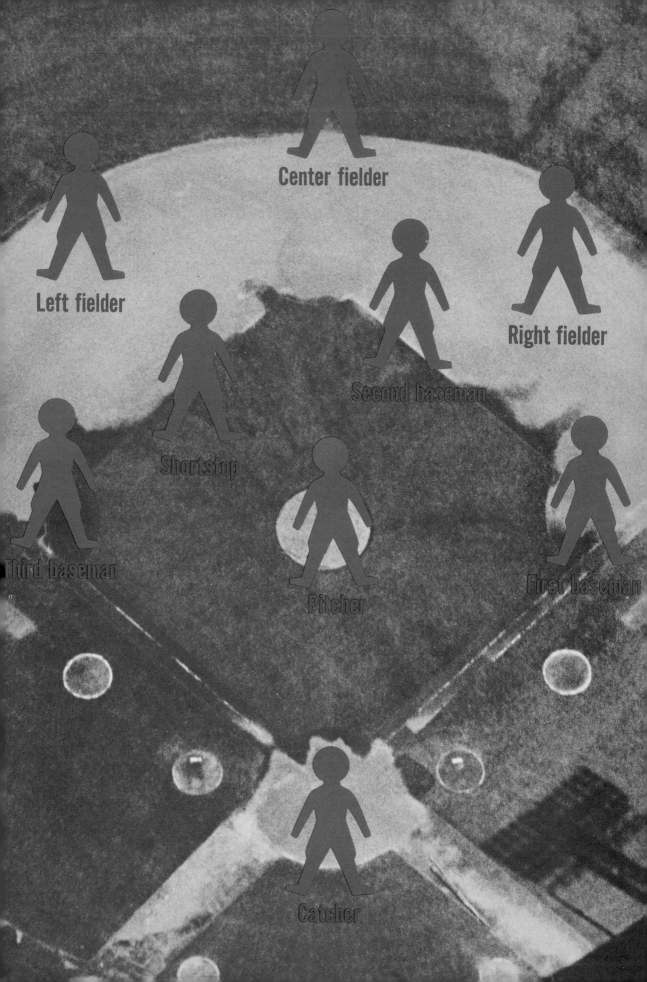

Where the team plays

The team at bat plays a simple position. Each batter hits in his own turn and runs the bases in progression from first to second to third and home. But what about the team in the field?

The first baseman plays behind the base, a little towards second. The second baseman plays between first and second. The shortstop plays between second and third. The third baseman plays behind third and a little towards second.

The right fielder is normally stationed between first and second and deep enough to catch long fly balls. The left fielder takes a similar position between second and third. The center fielder is positioned deep in the outfield directly behind second base.

The catcher, of course, is at home plate, directly behind the batter. Now notice the round area near the center of the diamond. That's where the pitcher stands.

When the pitcher throws to his catcher, the batter must try to hit the ball and get to first base safely without being put "out." But now what is all this about an "out"? When is a batter "out" and when is he "safe"?

"4 balls"

"walk"

Well, make believe you are the batter. You are stand-ing alongside of home plate. The pitcher throws the ball to his catcher, but it passes high over your head so that you couldn't hit it if your bat were as long as a telephone pole. Would that be fair? Of course not. That's why the rules say you do not have to swing at such bad pitches.

Bad pitches are called "balls," and if the pitcher throws four such bad pitches, you are allowed to go to first base safely. When you go to first base because the pitcher has thrown four "balls," that is called get-ting a "walk."

But suppose the pitcher throws the ball so that it passes across home plate somewhere between your knees and your shoulders. Certainly you should be able to hit that.

You swing the bat. Swoosh. You missed! Are you out? No. You are only out when you have missed for the third time. You are out if you have swung three times and missed, or even if you did not swing but three pitches have passed through the strike zone. Four balls and you walk—three strikes and you're out.

Of course now that you know about batting you won't always miss. Suppose you hit the pitch.

"3 strikes"

"ball one"

"grounder"

"fly ball"

The batted ball might go up in the air or it might roll along the ground. If it's a grounder and rolls out of the boundary of the playing field before it reaches first or third base you cannot run. It is called a "foul ball" and it is just a strike.

Or if, on its first bounce, a fly ball falls anywhere at all outside of the playing field, that is a foul ball, and a strike, too.

The best thing about this is that only the first two foul balls count as strikes. After that, you can hit all the foul balls you like without being called out. There's one exception... if you try to bunt after two strikes, you are out if the ball rolls foul.

But you're still up at bat and here comes the pitch. Smash. You hit it up in the air. Here comes a fielder under the ball. He catches it before it hits the ground. Sorry, Riley. You're out.

After the other eight men on the team have had their chance to bat, it's your turn again. This time you hit a grounder between first and second. Off you go toward first base as fast as your flying feet will carry you. But the shortstop has scooped up the ball and throws it to the first baseman. It gets there before you. Sorry, Riley. Out again.

"foul ball"

"safe"

How "outs" are made

Now you have discovered the three main ways in which outs are made:

1 You are out when you strike out.

2 You are out if a fielder catches a fly ball before it hits the ground.

3 You are out if a fielder with the ball tags you or the base before you get there.

The best thing a batter can do is to hit the ball so far that the fielders cannot catch it and get it back to home plate before he circles all the bases. This is called a "home run." But even the greatest baseball players don't usually hit home runs.

Suppose you walk...or beat the ball to one of the bases. Then it is up to your teammates to advance you around the bases. The goal of a good baseball player should be to try to get to base safely by any means he can and depend on the rest of the team to try to do the same.

Baseball is a team game that can only be won when all nine men on the team are doing their best. It cannot be won by one man alone, no matter how good he might seem to be.

Sliding and running bases

What do you know about baseball so far?

You know how to catch, how to throw, how to hit, how outs are made, and how runs are scored. You also know how to play the game, and how teams change after three outs until each team has had at least nine chances to bat.

Every player in the game has his chance to bat, and one thing every batter should know is the best way to run the bases to beat the ball to the bag.

When running to first base, the first baseman does not have to tag you. All he has to do is catch the ball and touch the base before you get there to make an out. To get to first base safely you just have to run as fast as you can.

But suppose a runner is already safe on first and wants to try to get to second base? He is not "forced" to go to second, because he can always choose to return to first. But the moment he makes a try for an extra base, he must be tagged with the ball by one of the fielders in order to be out. Even if he decided to return to first, he must be tagged. Of course, only one runner is allowed to occupy a base at a time.

How does a runner avoid being tagged? By sliding. Sliding doesn't get you to the base any faster, but it makes it more difficult for the fielder to touch you with the ball.

Watch how Riley does it.

Running for the bag, he has to beat the tag.

As the second baseman leaps for the ball, Riley starts to fall away.

In safely! See how his outstretched hand cushioned his fall. And see how his foot has hooked the outside corner of the bag, leaving only the smallest and most difficult area for a tag.

Being able to slide properly is worth practicing. It can mean the difference between a one-base hit and a two-base hit, and that small difference can often mean the difference between winning and losing the game.

The double play

Just as a batter would rather make a home run or three-base hit or two-base hit than a single, the fielding team would rather make three outs or two outs on a play than just a single out.

Making three outs at one time (called a triple play) is very rare. But most good fielding teams will make one or more two-out plays (double plays) during a ball game.

Sometimes a double play is made by one fielder alone. Suppose you were the second baseman and the batting team had a runner on first base. If the next batter hit a fly ball right at you and you caught it, he would be out. And if you tagged the runner while he was off base, he would be out, too. Double play.

But most double plays are the result of team-work.

Watch how it is done...

As a ground ball is hit on the right side of the infield, the batter starts for first base while the runner on first heads for second.

Quickly the second baseman scoops up the ball...

He throws to the shortstop, who has come over to cover second. The ball beats the runner to the base. One out.

When the ball is hit to the right side, it is fielded by the second baseman, first baseman, pitcher, or catcher (whoever can get to it first) while the shortstop covers second base.

The shortstop throws the ball to first. Success! The ball gets there before the batter does. Two outs. A quick double play.

Similarly, when the ball is hit to the left side, it is fielded by the pitcher, catcher, shortstop, or third baseman, while the second baseman covers the bag to relay the ball to first.

Look easy?

It is. But only after the fielders have mastered the skills of catching and throwing and have learned to work together as a team.

The curve ball

Baseball, as you can see, is a duel between the batter, who is trying to reach base to score a run, and the pitcher of the opposing team, who is trying to keep him from hitting the ball at all.

To become a good pitcher it is necessary to develop control so that you can throw the ball exactly where you want to each time. A very good pitcher will also be able to throw the ball fast and be able to make it curve when he wants to.

There is no great secret to the curve ball. Don't expect to be able to make a ball curve the first time you try. But once you know how it is done, you will be able to throw curves with only a little concentrated practice.

Batter   **Pitcher**

Ever see a boomerang spin out and curve around right back to where it came from? A baseball can be made to curve the same way—by spinning it.

How do you spin a baseball to make it curve? Why, just the opposite way you spin it to make it go straight, of course. The best way to see this is to watch Riley do it with a card. Then <u>you</u> do it with a card—do it until you learn the wrist and body movements.

Riley holds the card as he would a baseball, with his first two fingers spread slightly apart and thumb on the bottom.

Here he throws a straight ball...

Now he will go through the motions of throwing a straight ball. Here he goes, ready to throw.

See how he has let the card go from right in front of him. The whole front of his body is facing the catcher.

...a curve ball

This time, when Riley goes through the curve-ball motion, he will hold onto the card to demonstrate the difference. See how he starts out the same way.

This time, however, as he brings the card down, he starts to twist his body...and snap his wrist.

Look at the last picture and then look at his straight ball motion on the page facing. See how his wrist has twisted so that his thumb is now on top facing the camera? And see how his body has twisted so that his right shoulder is now lower than his left?

The twisting of the body and the sudden snapping of the wrist are the motions that give the ball enough spin to make it curve.

Some people think that you have to hold a ball a special way to make it curve. This is not true. Some pitchers, however, will hold a fast ball right on the seams... and hold the curve ball slightly off on the side of the seams to give them something to push against to help the spin.

Three
basic things
to know

1 Hold the ball loosely and let the
middle finger do all the work.

2 Don't just twist, but
snap the wrist suddenly at the very
last minute before letting the ball go.

3 Follow through with your body for added
spin so that your throwing shoulder
ends up lower than your rear shoulder.

There is also a fourth thing. Many ballplayers
learn to throw all sorts of good curve balls, but
never end up as pitchers.

The most important thing is to learn how to control a straight ball—to make it go just where you
want it most of the time. And a curve ball is use-
less unless you can control it the same way, too.

Now that you know all about curves, see if you can follow the curve on this ball. There it goes...

Is it going on the wrong side of the batter?...

Oooops, looks like it's starting to curve...

Coming down across the plate now, and the batter's getting ready to swing...

Oh, oh, it's going outside home plate...man, that curve was too big. Into the dirt for a ball. Curves, you see, can't be too hard. Riley learned to throw one just the way you did.

Now you know most of the essential things about baseball, and with a little practice you will learn to master them.

Besides the basic rules of the game, you know:

How to throw

How to catch

How to hit

How to bunt

How to slide and run bases

How to make a double play

How to throw a curve ball

But ...

the most important thing of all

is something that cannot be found in any book. It is called team spirit.

You must have what is called the "will to win." This means not only being a good sport, but being willing to do everything in your power and to the best of your abilities to help your team, for—as we have noted—baseball is a team game. Players with enough team spirit—with enough determination to win—have become champions even though they were not as good as many others in hitting and fielding.

So now that you know about the most important thing:

play ball!

N